Original title:
Sapling Serenades

Copyright © 2025 Creative Arts Management OÜ
All rights reserved.

Author: Gideon Barrett
ISBN HARDBACK: 978-1-80567-214-2
ISBN PAPERBACK: 978-1-80567-513-6

In the Embrace of the Earth

Tiny sprouts peek from the ground,
Wearing hats of dirt, they look quite round.
They wiggle and giggle, oh what a sight,
In muddy puddles, they dance with delight.

Rain clouds chuckle as they start to drip,
The plants rejoice, it's a wet little trip.
With each raindrop, they bounce and sway,
Making mud pies for the sunny day.

Flickers of Green Dreams

Little leaves whisper secrets round,
Telling tales of worms they found.
The sunbeams tickle, the shadows play,
As they plot the best lies to tell on a sunny day.

Grasshoppers join the jumping spree,
While ladybugs laugh, "Look at me!"
With a hop and a skip, they wiggle around,
In this green circus, joy is profound.

Garden of Harmonious Beginnings

Every flower prances in the breeze,
Dressed in colors, looking to please.
Bees buzz louder, overstepping their bounds,
Stealing sweet nectar, yet making no sounds.

The daisies argue, "Who's the best?"
While roses roll their eyes at the jest.
In this garden, laughter blooms loud,
A riot of colors, as dreams are avowed.

The Rhythm of Rooted Dreams

Roots tickle deep, a lively dance,
As worms wiggle and twirl in trance.
The soil sings low, a bassy sound,
While hopeful seedlings map dreams on the ground.

A squirrel scampers with a nut in tow,
Humming a tune as he darts to and fro.
In the rhythm of nature, funny things thrive,
In this grassy stage, all are alive.

Swaying Melodies of Wild Blossoms

In the garden, blooms are jiving,
With a breeze, they're high-fiving.
Butterflies dance, oh what a sight,
  Petals twirl with pure delight.

Bees are buzzing, quite the crew,
  Wearing hats of pollen too!
A daffodil's twist is all the rage,
As daisies moonwalk, center stage.

The Brightness of Budding Futures

Tiny sprouts with dreams so wide,
Chasing rainbows from inside.
Wiggling roots, they can't sit still,
Jumping up for every thrill.

With sunbeam smiles, they play their part,
Sprouting giggles from the heart.
Each morning dew, a belly laugh,
Nature's path—a funny path!

Voices of the Earth's New Children

Little leaves with jokes to share,
Tickling branches, what a flare!
Whispering winds, a playful tease,
Sharing secrets with the trees.

Young acorns rolling on the ground,
Cracking jokes, a silly sound.
Every shroom a comedian bright,
Tickling your toes, pure delight!

Songs of Life in Sunlit Spaces

In the sun, the flowers sing,
Bouncing tunes on vibrant spring.
Clovers laugh as they shoot up high,
Golden rays and giggles fly.

Worms in soil with a rhythm beat,
Dancing underground on tiny feet.
While ladybugs boast in the light,
Life's a party, what a sight!

Serenade for the Newborn Trees

In the garden, tiny trunks sway,
Chasing shadows, laughing all day.
Worms throw a party, soil's the stage,
Roots dance beneath, like a leaf-age mage.

Sunlight tickles, leaves begin to giggle,
Pests try to bug them, but trees just wiggle.
A squirrel named Nutty brings nuts to share,
All join the feast, not a worry or care.

Rhythms of Verdant Beginnings

Tiny buds burst with all their might,
Sprouts have dreams of reaching new height.
Breeze plays the drums, flowers hum along,
Bees bring the beat; oh, what a song!

Sticks join in, prancing with flair,
Dancers unite, roots hang in the air.
A raccoon with rhythm jigs to the beat,
While ants form a line, feeling the heat.

Odes to the Freshly Sprouted

Fresh shoots pop up like surprise balloons,
Under the sky, they flap like cartoons.
Grass stains giggle, mud pouts with glee,
As dear little sprouts shout, "Come dance with me!"

A crow shows off, strutting with pride,
While butterflies whirl, joining the ride.
Dewdrops laugh, giving hints of cheer,
"Look at us shine, oh saplings, my dear!"

Nature's Chorus: The Growing Season

A chorus of leaves begins to quip,
As sunlight pours, they laugh on a trip.
Clouds make faces, they puff up with grace,
While critters play tag, each finds their place.

Laughter echoes through branches so wide,
Silly seedlings roll, no need to hide.
Together they sway, a funny parade,
In this vibrant world, no fears are made.

Anthem of the Growing Green

In my garden, plants do dance,
Wiggling roots in a wild romance.
They giggle as the raindrops fall,
Bouncing leaves echoing their call.

Sunflowers stretch, trying to wave,
Competing to see who's the bravest knave.
Daisies roll on the soft, warm ground,
Laughing at the worms that abound.

The carrots wear their leafy hats,
Pretending to be royal cats.
Peppers prance in their bright attire,
Celebrating spring with a dance of fire.

So join this leafy, joyful crew,
Where every sprout has fun to do.
The garden's full of laughter, cheer,
With a chase of bugs that bring us near.

Crescendo of the Flourishing Seedlings

Tiny sprouts with giggly grins,
Whisper secrets as the fun begins.
A breeze tickles their tiny stems,
Encouraging their leafy whims.

Buds bounce around with silly flair,
Taking turns to rock the air.
They play hide and seek with the sun,
In this garden, everyone's having fun!

Petunias sway in a funny jig,
While daisies hop like a jumping pig.
A chorus of colors, they sing out loud,
In the heart of this vibrant crowd.

So if you stroll by this joyful patch,
Watch for giggles, that's the catch!
Nature's show is never quite bland,
Join the seedlings, give a hand!

Whims of the Wildflowers

Dandelions giggle in the breeze,
With crowns of fluff that tease.
Petunias prance in bright parade,
While daisies play a game of charade.

Buttercups blushing with delight,
Whisper silly secrets at night.
Tulips twist in a jolly jig,
As bees join in, doing a little dig.

Lavender laughs with fragrant sighs,
Sharing jokes with butterflies.
Poppies pop up with a cheer,
Saying, "Let's spread joy far and near!"

In this garden, mischief thrives,
With flowers living their vibrant lives.
Their dance is silly, wild, and free,
Oh what a sight for all to see!

The Sigh of Seedlings

Tiny sprouts stretch in morning light,
Winking at worms with delight.
With sunflower hats so tall and grand,
They prank the raindrops, making a stand.

Carrots chuckle beneath the ground,
As zucchinis share laughs all around.
Lettuce leaves ruffle in playful delight,
While peas giggle in their green little flight.

Radishes blush with a rooty grin,
Rooting for friends, where to begin?
Beets have a dance, round and round,
While turnips just roll on the ground.

Each tiny seed has a tale to tell,
Making the garden a jolly hotel.
With laughter growing, oh what a sight,
In the shade of the stars, they shine so bright!

Murmurs from the Forest's Edge

At the forest's edge, the bushes croak,
With branches that laugh and poke.
A squirrel tells tales of nutty fun,
While birds chirp songs 'til the day is done.

The ferns wave hello with a graceful shake,
As raccoons play peek-a-boo by the lake.
Mushrooms giggle in their spot,
Hiding secrets they've always got.

Trees gossip softly under their leaves,
As the wind carries whispers like thieves.
A fox dons a hat made of twigs,
While crickets strum tunes that dance and twigs.

Every rustle brings merriment near,
As the forest laughs, loud and clear.
In the wild, the world is so light,
Where every creature is a delight!

Serenade of Shade

Beneath the canopy, where giggles play,
The sunbeams caper, oh what a day!
Lizards lounge in a lazy spree,
While shadows dance with glee, oh me!

The trees perform a dramatic flair,
Waving branches in the warm air.
Toads croak jokes that make leaves shake,
While squirrels tumble and bump with a quake.

A picnic with ants in a scrumptious row,
Sharing crumbs from above, don't they glow?
The laughter echoes 'neath foliage green,
Where the fun is ripe and the joy is seen.

In this shade where laughter thrives,
The spirit of playtime truly arrives.
Nature's stage is set with delight,
In a serenade that feels just right!

The Sweetness of Saplings

In the breeze, young leaves dance,
They sway and twirl in a leafy chance.
A squirrel slips on a clumsy climb,
Nature's laughter, pure and sublime.

Tiny branches hold dreams so bright,
Whispering secrets in morning light.
A bee trips over petals, oh what a sight,
Nature's humor shines, taking flight.

Nature's Gentle Anthem

The birds sing songs with quite the flair,
A worm gets groovy without a care.
Down by the brook, frogs leap and croak,
Each note a giggle, a gentle poke.

The daisies nod in floral delight,
As ants march in a perfect line, tight.
They trip on a twig — oh, what a plight!
A symphony of chaos, nature's invite.

Embers of Spring Tones

The sun peeks out with a shy, warm grin,
While daisies blossom, let the fun begin.
A dandelion wiggles, just for kicks,
As butterflies practice their aerial tricks.

Grasshoppers jump with style and grace,
But land on a snail — oh, what a race!
Nature's folly, a playful embrace,
Bringing laughter to this green place.

Cradle of Awakening Woods

In the forest, secrets softly breathe,
Where mushrooms giggle beneath the leaves.
A raccoon wearing a mask, oh so sly,
Steals berries while birds roll their eye.

Trees tell stories of silly old times,
With knots and bends – nature's wise rhymes.
Whispering laughter in the gentle climbs,
A playful tale wrapped in leafy chimes.

Earthen Whispers

In the garden, dirt's a friend,
Telling tales that never end.
Worms dance with all their might,
Raining giggles in the light.

Plants gossip 'neath the sun,
Joking how they just had fun.
Roots tap-dance in the soil,
Living life without the toil.

Birds crack jokes up in the trees,
Tickling branches with the breeze.
Frogs croak laughs, it's quite absurd,
Fluffy clouds nod at each word.

With every sprout, a chuckle shares,
Laughter floats on gentle airs.
Nature's humor, bright and spry,
Creatures giggle as they pass by.

Swells of Life

Bubbles pop in dew-soaked morn,
Little leaves feel quite reborn.
Silly ants march to a beat,
Twirling petals at their feet.

Sprouts rise tall in the bright sun,
Tickled by the breeze, it's fun.
Fungus wiggles, mushrooms grin,
Together they spin tales within.

A sunflower leans to peek,
At a snail that's lost its streak.
'Hey slowpoke, are you alive?'
They laugh, the dreams they'll derive.

Pumpkins joke about their weight,
Growing double—I can't wait!
On the vine, they roll and sway,
Life's a joke, come laugh and play!

The Serenity of Sprouting

In the soil, the giggles grow,
Beneath the earth, they steal the show.
Tiny seeds dream big and loud,
Stretching tall, all proud and cowed.

Sunbeams tickle every sprout,
While the daisies dance about.
Bees buzz jokes from flower to flower,
Humor blooms in every hour.

The roots conspire, twist, and twirl,
Grassy tufts in a laugh unfurl.
With each shake and sway, they cheer,
Tickled by the clouds so near.

As gentle breezes flair and tease,
Little leaves dance with such ease.
Nature plays a game of tease,
Sprouting joy among the trees.

Young Leaves in Reverie

A tender sprout with vivid dreams,
Whispers secrets, playful schemes.
In the orchard's lively hum,
Giggling leaves show where they're from.

Squirrels leap, a nutty show,
Clouds join in a fluffy row.
Little buds stand side by side,
Chortling as they choose to hide.

Dancing rays of sunlight bright,
Wave and flirt, take wing in flight.
Acorns crack jokes from the ground,
While nature's laughter spins around.

Cherubs shower down their cheer,
As grasshoppers jump with glee near.
Every leaf a funny tale,
In the garden, laughter's trail.

Crescendo of New Life

In a pot, a tiny sprout,
Grew a face, I swear, a shout!
With each drop of rain it drank,
It danced as if it knew it stank.

Roots are wriggling, what a sight,
Making friends with worms each night!
The leaves are giggling, what a tease,
Waving to the buzzing bees.

Sunshine comes, it drinks with glee,
Sipping tea, oh so carefree!
A garden party soon in place,
With carrots sporting quite the face.

The Playful Breeze of Blossoms

A dandelion, a fluffy clown,
Wobbling wildly, wearing a crown.
"Blow on me!" it shouts with flair,
And puffs out seeds to fill the air.

The tulips wear their bright best gear,
Doing the salsa, oh dear, oh dear!
With daffodils, they form a band,
Creating tunes across the land.

The pansy winks, the marigolds cheer,
As petals twirl, no hint of fear.
While bumblebees swing their best moves,
The crowd of petals groves and grooves.

The Unfolding Poem of Nature

A tiny seedling dreams of fame,
Soon to be a leafy game!
With every inch, it takes a shot,
For selfies in the garden plot.

The sunbeams tickle every leaf,
Creating giggles, quite the relief.
With ladybugs, it spins around,
In poetry, joy can be found.

As blooms break free from slumber's clasp,
They giggle 'til laughter's a gasp.
The trees join in, their bows so grand,
Choreographing nature's band.

Awakenings of the Woodland

In the woods, the mushrooms sway,
Thinking they're the stars of the play.
With deer who prance and squirrels that sing,
It's a woodland dance, oh what a fling!

The brook babbles jokes, and frogs croak along,
Each ripple a note in their morning song.
The raccoons don masks, so sly, so neat,
Having a ball with berries to eat.

The owl hoots softly, "What's the fuss?"
While crickets chirp, they join in a plus.
As dawn stretches wide on a bright green sheet,
Nature's a jester, oh, what a treat!

Tones of Tender Newness

In the garden, a sprout takes a bow,
Singing loudly, 'Look at me now!'
A tiny sunflower, loud as a drum,
Tickles the daisies, saying, 'Come, come!'

The carrots giggle, their tops in the air,
While broccoli jokes, 'I've got good hair!'
The radish rolls over, all snug in the dirt,
'Let's start a band, and wear cool shirts!'

A little green pea in a pod found its groove,
Dancing with roots, they just can't lose!
"Oh what a party, let's all take a chance!
The world's our stage, now let's do the prance!"

With laughter and cheer, sprouts brightly sway,
In tones of green, they sing every day!

Whispers in the Woodlands

In the shadows of tall trees, seedlings convene,
Plotting their takeover of the unseen!
A wise old fern says, 'Just be profound,
And remember to grow with your roots in the ground!'

An oak tree chuckles, 'Kids, take a seat,
Life's but a circle, so just don't repeat!'
A jolly old stump tells a pun so grand,
'Why did the twig leave? It couldn't stand!'

Through rustling leaves, the whispers fly,
"I'm rooted in humor, just give it a try!"
A nightingale joins with a tune full of charm,
Singing of saplings, who sow jokes like a farm!

At dusk, the woodlands laugh and play,
Giving thanks for another delightful day!

Canopy Crescendos

Under a canopy, young buds collide,
Making up lyrics as they giggle and glide.
A chirpy grasshopper leaps with delight,
'Join our concert! It starts at twilight!'

The willow whispers, 'Hey, check out my sway,
I'm the coolest dancer in the fray!'
While mushrooms chime in with a cheeky grin,
'Try to out-fungus me? Where to begin?'

Crickets provide a catchy beat,
While snails groove slowly, no time for defeat.
'Slide into the rhythm, don't lose your way,
We're the stars of the forest cabaret!'

With the moon above, they gather in cheer,
Nature's own concert, oh, what a sphere!

The Birth of Young Flora

In the soil, a new bloom starts to squawk,
'Hey everyone, it's time for a talk!'
A budding tulip says, 'Ahem, lend me your ear,
Why did the flower never show fear?'

'Because it knew its petals were meant to shine,
While dreaming of rainbows, pinks, and divine!'
Then daisies chime in, 'What's a bud's favorite sport?
Playing on stems, we're the cutest court!'

Little violets giggle, all snug in a patch,
With pansies preparing a colorful match.
'Let's paint the garden in colors so bright,
We'll bring all the critters to marvel at night!'

Their laughter echoes, through the fields they prance,
In the birth of young flora, it's always a dance!

Melodies Beneath the Canopy

In the shade, a squirrel prances,
Nuts in hand, he takes his chances.
Leaves are giggling in the breeze,
While branches sway like dancing trees.

A raccoon sings a loony tune,
Underneath the bright full moon.
With every note, the birds take flight,
Joining in with pure delight.

The mushrooms clap, their caps aglow,
To the rhythm of the winds that blow.
Nature's band is quite the sight,
As giggles echo through the night.

So if you hear a rustle near,
Don't fret, it's just the woods in cheer.
The forest's laughter fills the air,
With melodies beyond compare.

Dance of the Tender Stems

Little sprouts in a line so neat,
Twist and turn, they dance on their feet.
A gentle breeze spins them around,
In a waltz upon the ground.

Dandelions join in with a puff,
With their seeds, it's all in good fun.
Wobbling as bees buzz by,
They sway and stretch toward the sky.

A caterpillar taps a toe,
In a rhythm that starts off slow.
But soon he's grooving, what a sight!
A belly dance in morning light.

When branches laugh and roots agree,
Nature's dance is wild and free.
With every wiggle and jump they make,
The ground beneath begins to shake.

Symphonies of New Growth

Shoots of green with giggles sprout,
Making sounds that twist about.
A whispering leaf leaves a joke,
While a sleepy slug starts to poke.

With every bud, a chuckle blooms,
In the heart of all the looms.
Flowers wink, exchanging grins,
As sunlight tickles all their skins.

A worm on stilts can't find his way,
Stumbling through the grass at play.
The earthworms laugh; they roll in glee,
In this garden's merry spree.

From every nook, a tune arises,
As critters join in, much to surprises.
The symphonies of joy do swell,
In nature's grand, enchanting spell.

Chants of the Morning Dew

Morning dew, a glittering mist,
To take a sip, the critters insist.
Each drop a giggle, a tiny voice,
As blades of grass rejoice by choice.

A feathered friend hops with delight,
Sipping drops as a morning rite.
With each fresh drop, they sing their cheer,
Creating a chorus for all to hear.

Butterflies flutter, a vibrant parade,
Beneath the dew, a dance is played.
They twist and twirl with such finesse,
In morning charm, they look to impress.

When sunlight beams begin to break,
The dewy voices softly shake.
A final farewell, as warmth sets in,
But the laughter lingers, like a playful grin.

Harmony of Roots

In the soil, they wiggle and play,
Whispering secrets all day.
With tangled toes, they deeply dwell,
Creating chaos, oh what a smell!

They gossip about the sun's bright rays,
And laugh at shadows that come in arrays.
With every inch, they poke and prod,
Their mother trees laugh, 'Oh what a squad!'

A noodle dance is what they do,
Stretching in soil, like gooey stew.
"Did you hear the joke from the wind?"
Roots whisper softly, "Let's pretend!"

While raindrops tickle with a splash,
And worms join in for a muddy bash.
With roots so spry and hearts so bold,
They sing of mischief, stories untold!

The Dance of Tiny Branches

Oh tiny branches, bend and sway,
In the breeze, they find their play.
They twist and twirl, a joyful bunch,
With leaves like hats, they munch and crunch.

On a party night under the moon,
They groove to the nightbirds' lilting tune.
"Who's the best dancer?" they all cheer,
The one with the sparkles, oh so dear!

A squirrel joins with a cheeky grin,
Challenging branches, let's spin to win!
With a flip and a flap, they take to the sky,
Making the flowers giggle as they pass by.

But watch your step, dear feathered friend,
These branches have jokes that never end.
Peeking out with a chuckling leaf,
They know, oh yes, humor is their belief!

First Light through Tender Foliage

In the morning, a glow so bright,
Foliage giggles at the sight.
"Hello sun, you've come to play,
Let's catch the bugs before they sway!"

With dew drops dancing on each leaf,
They whisper secrets, beyond belief.
"Do you see that cloud? What a silly shape,
Looks like a cat in a nature cape!"

The flowers join in, flaunting colors bold,
Trading compliments like they're made of gold.
"Your petals shine, just like my dreams,
Let's dance together by the sparkling streams!"

With light filtering through, they sway in delight,
Creating shadows that wiggle tight.
"Wake up world, our time is now,
We'll sprinkle joy, oh yes, and how!"

A Symphony of Sprouts

A little sprout sprouted one day,
He wiggled and jiggled in his own way.
"Hey there, friend, come join the groove,
A symphony of sprouts, let's all move!"

Next to him, a pea pod cheered,
"Count me in, I'm feeling weird!"
With a hop and a bop, they started to sing,
Creating a melody, oh what a fling!

Carrot tops danced, full of glee,
"Don't forget us, we're here, you see!"
They formed a band with leafies bold,
Making music from stories of old.

With every note, the garden would sway,
Turning the dull into a bright display.
"A little soil can make us sprout,
Join the fun, let's twist and shout!"

Treetop Dreams in a Gentle Breeze

In the branches, dreams take flight,
Squirrels dance, oh what a sight!
Leaves giggle in the warm sunlight,
Wishing clouds would toss a kite.

Birds gossip in whispers soft,
While ants march, their spirits aloft.
"Who's that sapling? Is he tough?"
The oak just laughs, "You're all too rough!"

The breeze tickles each swaying leaf,
Nature plays, beyond belief.
Watch the blossoms waltz and sway,
Beneath the sun's warm, golden ray.

Treetops burst with playful glee,
Join the fun, come climb with me!
Life's a jest among the greens,
Nature's jokes are the best of scenes.

Gentle Murmurs of the Young Grove

In the grove where young trees stand,
They whisper secrets, oh so grand!
"Did you hear that? I felt a breeze!"
"Of course, it's just the ants with tease!"

Saplings chuckle, trying to grow,
"Why so tall?" they ask the crow.
"Because I have style," he says with pride,
While shadowed branches mock and bide.

A butterfly flutters through the scene,
"Oh look, it's a flying jellybean!"
What's next, they wonder, a dancing pie?
The oak just sighs, "I should comply."

Every rustle brings a grin,
With each breeze, the laughter spins.
Nature's mirth blooms bright and clear,
Join the chorus, lend an ear!

Ballad of the Flourishing Foliage

Leaves are singing in the sun,
This grove's a party, oh what fun!
Dancing shadows sway in cheer,
"Watch out, here comes the deer!"

Roots are tapping, getting spry,
While squirrels zip and zoom on by.
"Join the hoedown while you can!"
Said the tallest, barker of the clan.

Toadstools nod with joyful grace,
Their hats flopping all over the place.
Whispers of laughter fill the air,
"Is that a groan? Or just a hare?"

Buds are bursting with delight,
As fireflies flicker in the night.
Under silver moonlit glow,
Nature's dance continues to flow.

The Awakening of Nature's Voices

Sunrise slips through leafy sighs,
Nature's chorus, oh how it flies!
"Here comes breakfast on a tray!"
"Hope it's worms," the robin brays.

Frogs croak loudly, kings of the pond,
"Be quiet, please!" the lilies respond.
A breeze whispers jokes, old and new,
While daisies giggle, "Who are you?"

Breezy lullabies stir awake,
Rabbits hop, making the ground shake.
"Don't forget to mind your feet!"
Said the hedgehog, too cool to eat.

The forest bursts with joyous sounds,
Every rustle, laughter bounds.
Nature wakes, and what a show,
Funny moments, seeds to sow!

Underneath the Emerging Sky

Underneath the big, blue dome,
Tiny seeds dream of their home.
Wiggly worms dance all around,
While roots play hide and seek in the ground.

A dandelion whispers jokes so sly,
While laughing leaves aim for the sky.
The sun giggles, bright and warm,
As nature's crew goes out to perform.

From acorns small to towering trees,
Each one tells a tale with ease.
The squirrels are acrobats on the chase,
While bees buzz in a whirl and a race.

A property of laughter, nature's cheer,
With every bloom, there's more to hear.
As branches sway to a foolish tune,
Underneath the sun, we all are in bloom.

Blossoms in the Breeze

Blossoms spin like twirling tops,
As petals fall and giggle, 'Oops!'
The grass blades sway, all in delight,
While butterflies play tag in flight.

A critter hops and trips on dew,
With pollen stuck like yellow glue.
The daisies point and proudly boast,
'We're the stars, let's make a toast!'

The wind transforms into a friend,
Telling jokes that never end.
A rose blushes, thinking it's sly,
As clouds burst out laughing nearby.

In this garden, joy's the creed,
With every sprout, a brand-new deed.
So, raise a leaf and join the glee,
Let nature's humor set you free.

Cuddle of Earth and Sky

Roots and skies embrace so tight,
As stars giggle at silly sights.
The grass tickles little feet,
While raindrops fall, oh what a treat!

A cloud drizzles, a playful tease,
While trees sway like they're at a squeeze.
The sun peeks through with a big old grin,
Making sure the fun begins.

Bugs wear hats, oh what a show,
As ladybugs boast their tiny glow.
With each tickle from the breeze,
Nature's chorus sings with ease.

It's a cuddle, a big warm hug,
Where laughter sparks and hearts stay snug.
With every moment full of cheer,
The earth and sky make joy so clear.

A Lullaby for the Little Ones

Whispers of the night prepare for dreams,
As crickets chirp in playful schemes.
Stars wink down like cheeky sprites,
While shadows dance and take their flights.

Budding blooms hum soft and low,
Telling secrets only they know.
The moon grins, casting silver beams,
As crickets stitch together dreams.

Fireflies with their light so bright,
Paint the dark with pure delight.
A soft breeze rocks the world to sleep,
While night promises joy to keep.

So snuggle close, little one dear,
As nature's lullaby draws near.
With twinkling stars to light the way,
Rest your heart and let dreams play.

Serenade of Sunlight and Soil

In the garden, worms do dance,
Twisting, turning, in a trance.
Sunlight tickles on their backs,
As they plan their silly hacks.

Roots are chatting, pot to pot,
Gossip flowing, quite the plot.
"Did you hear?" a sproutlet sneaks,
"The daisies laughed for two whole weeks!"

Underneath the leafy green,
Little critters play unseen.
"More sun for me!" a flower pleads,
While laughing at the sassy weeds!

Composting jokes, they spread the cheer,
Nature's humor, loud and clear.
With each breeze, a chuckle flies,
The roots and shoots, oh what a surprise!

Fables of the Forest Floor

In the shadows, mushrooms bloom,
Whisper secrets, share some doom.
"Old Oak snored, fell fast asleep,
Gained a trunk while dreams ran deep!"

Acorns giggle, plop and drop,
Rolling around, they can't just stop.
"Catch me if you can, oh tree!"
Squirrels chase with wild glee.

Ladybugs in polka dots,
Hold a party with small tots.
Little ants march, take their chance,
Suddenly, they start to dance!

The dirt is rich with tales untold,
Laughter echoes, never old.
Fables woven in the clay,
Nature's humor marks the day!

The First Whisper of Leaves

As spring creeps in with leafy curls,
   Little birds share silly twirls.
"I lost my nest!" the sparrow cries,
And then they giggle, in disguise.

The branches stretch, they wave hello,
   To giggling buds in a row.
"I'm taller!" boasts the bravest pine,
But all agree, they're feeling fine.

Wind tickles leaves, they laugh so bright,
   Spinning around, what a sight!
A whirl of colors, joy's the theme,
Creating laughter like a dream!

With every rustle, secrets shared,
   A playful vibe fills the air.
The first whispers bring delight,
Nature's jesters, pure and light!

A Young Tree's Ballad

In a meadow, a young tree sways,
Dreaming of its youthful days.
"Look at me!" it lifts its limbs,
Listening to the playful whims.

Squirrels dash and play around,
Tickling roots beneath the ground.
"I'm the king of this tall patch!"
Barking dogs just watch and scratch.

Leaves do giggle in the breeze,
Whispering jokes with utmost ease.
"Have you heard the one about the sun?"
"Of course!" laugh the daisies, "That's the fun!"

Twirling slowly as the night falls,
Young tree hears nature's calls.
With every rustle, every cheer,
It sings its song, the world can hear!

The Harmony of Nature's Children

In the garden, ants do prance,
Singing songs of their last dance.
While daisies giggle in the breeze,
Tickled by the dancing bees.

Frogs hop on a lily pad,
Making music, oh so bad!
Their croaks are quite the silly sound,
While snails slide slowly 'round and 'round.

Up above, the birds jest,
Chirping tunes at nature's fest.
Each branch sways with leafy cheer,
As crickets join in, loud and clear.

Laughter echoes through the glade,
In this funny, leafy parade.
Nature's children play with glee,
In harmony, wild and free.

Chants of Leafy Beginnings

Little leaves whispering low,
'We're the stars of this show!'
With wiggles, giggles, they unfold,
Sharing secrets, stories told.

A wobbly worm takes the stage,
Recites lines with leafy rage.
'Oh, what fun to twist and squirm!'
As they nod to the dance with charm.

Raindrops bounce like playful friends,
Creating laughter that transcends.
They splash and shimmer on the ground,
While flowers twirl all around.

Sunlight peeks through branches green,
Painting shadows — what a scene!
Nature's choir begins to sing,
A joyful tune, oh what a fling!

Budding Melodies

In nursery beds, young sprouts do play,
Stretching leaves to greet the day.
With little giggles, they all cheer,
A symphony for all to hear.

A bunny hops through clover sprout,
Singing loud, there's never a doubt.
While petals spin in bright delight,
Swaying gently in the light.

Around the pond, the frogs reprise,
Their jumpy tunes, quite the surprise!
With every leap, a new refrain,
They croak and giggle in the rain.

The world's a stage for every bough,
Where nature's joys take a bow.
With laughter wrapped in every breeze,
These budding melodies aim to please.

Swaying in the Soft Wind

Dancing dandelions in a line,
Whisper secrets, oh so fine.
Sharing giggles with the grass,
As the breezes come to pass.

A wandering squirrel with a hat,
Sings a song that goes 'pitter pat'.
While robins do a cheeky jig,
Spinning 'round, out comes a twig!

As the sun dips low and wide,
Nature's children sway with pride.
Branches swing and leaves take flight,
Stargazing as day turns to night.

With every twirl, the laughter swells,
In a world where joy compels.
Swaying softly, they begin to rhyme,
In nature's dance, we lose all time.

Notes from the Blossoming Grove

In a grove where young trees play,
They dance each time the breezes sway.
One joked, 'I'm taller than a shoe!'
While others laughed, 'You wish you grew!'

A squirrel played the piano keys,
With acorns rolling down like leaves.
The trunks would sway, the branches clap,
Nature's rhythm in this leafy rap.

A bird popped by and said with glee,
'Look at me! I'm fancy-free!'
With feathers bright and cheeks so round,
It's the quirkiest show in town!

They sing beneath the shining sun,
Where roots entwine and laughter's spun.
Nature's humor, wild and free,
In this gown of green, we sing with glee!

Sprout Songs at Dawn

At the break of light, a giggle grows,
Tiny sprouts wear mud like clothes.
'Why'd the flower blush?' one asked,
'Cause it didn't want to be outclassed!'

The grass said, 'I'm the best dancer here!'
While a daisy declared, 'I have no fear!'
With every sway, they all agreed,
The simplest joys are what we need.

A worm wiggled, showing its flair,
'Worms get down, we don't care!'
The roots clapped in the soil's embrace,
A muddy dance with a smiling face.

In this morning fun, all is right,
The sprouts sing loud with sheer delight.
With petals wide and hearts so light,
They greet the day, oh what a sight!

Sonnet of Seedlings

In the garden where the laughter grows,
Young seedlings share their silly shows.
One claimed to sprout legs to run,
While others said, 'We just have fun!'

A beetle brought a tiny drum,
And danced around, 'Here I come!'
The plants all giggled, swayed a round,
In this patch where joy is found.

Like bouncing beans on a springy day,
They jump and jive in a leafy sway.
With sunshine smiles and roots entwined,
Their hearty tunes are sweetly kind.

So here among the greens so bright,
Let's laugh and frolic in pure delight.
For in this space, the cheer we share,
Transforms the air with friendship's care.

The Quietude of Young Trees

Amidst the grove, it starts to hum,
Whispers of bark, oh what a strum!
Tiny branches sway with pride,
'That breeze is mine!' they all decided.

A squirrel peeked, gave a cheesy grin,
'This tree's got moves! Let's all join in!'
With rustling leaves the giggling grew,
As birdies chirped a silly tune too.

Beneath the skyline, shadows play,
They ponder life in a breezy way.
In such calmness, laughter's delight,
Hiding giggles, tight and light.

So here's to the fun in every swirl,
Where young trees dance, and wonders unfurl.
In this peaceful space, joy's the key,
As nature sings in symphony.

Boughs in the Breeze

Tiny leaves dance, oh what a sight,
Swinging and swaying, with all their might.
They giggle and twist, as they catch the air,
Whispering secrets, without a care.

Buds poke their heads, peeking around,
Hiding from squirrels who leap and bound.
"No acorns for you!" the branches proclaim,
As the critters frolic, playing their game.

A breeze with a tickle, a flutter delight,
Branches get wobbly, oh what a fright!
Sticks that are older laugh with such glee,
"It's all in the dance, just trust it," they plea.

Roots below chuckle, they join in the fun,
Trying to stretch, but they weigh a ton.
"Next time we'll wiggle, just wait and you'll see,
When thorns learn to tango, we'll all be carefree!"

Awakening Earth

From under the soil, life starts to thrum,
Waking up gently, here they come!
Buds burst through with a pop and a cheer,
Saying, "Look out, springtime is here!"

Colors explode, it's a real party scene,
From bright golden daffodils to lush mossy green.
The worms are all dancing, a wriggly parade,
While ants carry lunch, oh the fun they've made!

With a push and a nudge, earth cracks with a laugh,
A dandelion giggles, "Hey, look at my staff!"
Bees buzz around, like a royal delight,
"Make way for the nectar, our future's so bright!"

Through all the laughs, nature's cheer carries on,
As seedlings poke out to join this joyful dawn.
Each sprout brings a smile, each bloom shows a grin,
Making the world feel like a whimsical spin!

Soft Voices of New Life

In a little green nook, the seedlings awake,
Chorusing softly, make no mistake.
Whispering dreams of fields far and wide,
While the earthworms sing, taking all in stride.

A seed and a sprout play peekaboo games,
"Bet you can't guess all our funny names!"
With roots that tickle, they giggle and glow,
Creating a ruckus, all hushing their show.

Raindrops fall gently, they jump in delight,
"Splash us some more, we'll dance through the night!"
The grasshoppers join in, with nimble feet,
Puppies join the jam, adding to the beat!

Nature's a stage with the best kind of cast,
Where laughter is endless, and good times are vast.
So gather round friends, with your watering can,
Let's shower our laughter, together we'll fan!

The Journey of Young Roots

Young roots venture out, with a curious flair,
Feeling their way, like they just don't care.
"Is this up, or down? Oh wait, let's go wide!"
They tangle and twist, on the slow, crazy ride.

"Watch out for rocks!" a wise elder yells,
"There's mud monsters lurking with magical spells!"
Roots hug the earth, then break into song,
"Join in our journey, it won't take long!"

The journey is wobbly but full of delight,
As roots scheme and dream, in the warm, soft night.
"Let's reach for the next snack, the juiciest one,
You bring the snacks, I'll bring the fun!"

So together they wriggle, pushing through clumps,
Finding their way, dancing over small lumps.
With each little inch, they giggle and cheer,
For roots know the secret, their destination is near!

Melodies of the Canopy

In the forest, leaves do sway,
Squirrels dance and then they play.
Birds are singing tunes so bright,
Bouncing on branches, what a sight!

One tree croaked a funny tune,
Bugs were buzzing, oh so soon.
A wooden flute from old man oak,
Had a laugh that made us choke!

With the sun high in the sky,
Little critters zooming by.
Dancing shadows on the floor,
Chirpy concerts we adore!

A twig took flight, just like a bird,
"Hey, look at me!" it chirped and stirred.
A parade of stems with flair,
What a show we've all laid bare!

The Awakening Boughs

Awake, awake, the trees do yawn,
Their branches stretch with every dawn.
A raccoon's hat, tipped just so,
Brings laughter loud wherever they go.

Mossy trolls with grins so wide,
Sing with flowers in the tide.
Dancing ants wear tiny shoes,
Stepping light, they have no blues.

Giggling leaves that twist and twirl,
In the breeze, they swirl and whirl.
"Watch my pirouette!" one shouts,
As playful wind begins to sprout!

All of nature joins the fun,
Squirrels conquer, trees will run.
Boughs with voices full of jest,
Who knew branches could be blessed?

Nursery Rhymes of Nature

Once there was a tiny seed,
Wiggling 'round with funny speed.
"Plant me here!" it gave a shout,
"Watch me grow, there's no doubt!"

Along came rain with splashes bright,
"Let's get dancing, oh what a sight!"
With puddles forming, frogs did leap,
Croaking rhymes, they wouldn't sleep.

A sunbeam tickled every leaf,
"Come play with us!"—no room for grief.
Caterpillars spun their tales,
On playful winds, they caught the gales.

Children of the woods unite,
With giggles echoing in delight.
Bouncing blossoms sing and rhyme,
In this place, we dance through time!

Gentle Breezes and Growing Greens

Breezes blow with laughter light,
Whispers soft and quite a sight.
Wiggly worms, a garden crew,
Dancing dirt, yes that's their view!

Leaves like hands that wave and greet,
Mice in shoes with little feet.
"Join our party, come along!"
The leafy choir sings a song.

Herbs and veggies cheer, rejoice,
Grasshoppers join and raise their voice.
With sprouts so tall in funny hats,
They sway around like playful brats!

Nature giggles, all in sync,
With every word, we dare to think.
In fields and woods, let's break the rules,
Silly nature, oh, how it cools!

Tales of Courage in the Garden

In the garden, a beet with a dream,
He lifted his leaves, thought he'd gleam,
But a rabbit exclaimed, "You're a snack,"
"I'll brave this diet attack!"

A tiny ant marched with pride,
Said, "Fear me, for I have no ride!"
But a raindrop splashed, oh what fun,
Now I'm a pool, not just one!"

The sunflower swayed, claimed a throne,
With petals like crowns, bright as stone,
But the breeze just laughed and clung tight,
"You're a tall joke; watch me take flight!"

And there sat a worm, full of tales,
Whispering secrets of snails and snails,
They chuckled through roots under the grass,
"Courage grows funny; let's raise a glass!"

The Quiet Growth of Tomorrow

A seedling stretched, said, "Look at me!"
"I'm destined for grandiosity!"
But a slug just slid by, gave a wink,
"Your future's more sticky than you think!"

The sun shone bright, but then a cloud,
Rained on the dreams of the proud,
A dandelion puffed with glee,
"Let's float our lives, so carefree!"

A tiny sprout dreamed of height,
While a gopher plotted with delight,
"You'll be my snack if I get through!"
"But I'll grow fast, it's a race, boo-hoo!"

Though quiet the growth, there's laughs in the fray,
Each plant has a story, its own funny way,
In the garden where giggles and roots intertwine,
Tomorrow's growth is a riot with sunshine!"

Illumination of New Canopies

A tree thought to don a bright hat,
"Watch me dazzle, I'll shine like a cat!"
But the wind just howled with a grin,
"Dear friend, you're losing—where to begin?"

The branches below were plotting their rise,
But a squirrel just peeked with wide eyes,
"If I pretend to be you from above,
Will anyone notice this nutty love?"

A beech whispered sweet to the oak,
"How do you manage, are you a joke?"
The oak just chuckled, thick with glee,
"I'm wise enough to sway and be free!"

So new canopies grew with laughter quite clear,
Each leaf danced along, and the critters drew near,
In nature's embrace, under skies wide and blue,
Every shenanigan blooms; oh, how they grew!"

Nature's Infant Songs

A tiny seed hummed a curious tune,
While crickets joined in, under the moon,
"Let's tap dance tonight, just for fun!"
And the flowers joined in, one by one!

A bee buzzed in, swaying around,
"Who's got the moves? I'm nature-bound!"
The daisies giggled, swaying with ease,
"Follow the beat of the buzzing breeze!"

The clouds above made a soft pillow,
As the wind played music on leaves so mellow,
"Nature's concert, what a grand sight!"
The trees echoed back, dancing through the night!

With laughter and songs, the garden would bloom,
Each little creature found room to zoom,
In this lively choir, oh so spry,
Every cheerful tune under the sky!"

Whispers of New Growth

Tiny leaves giggle in the breeze,
Jumping on branches with such ease.
Roots play hide and seek below,
Wishing they'd sprout and steal the show.

A worm wears glasses, reading the plot,
While ants dance around, giving it all they've got.
The sun winks at the playful sprout,
As raindrops cheer, there's no doubt.

Squirrels chase shadows, trying to climb,
Accidentally tripping on nature's thyme.
Each whisper of growth seems to sing,
A concert for all of spring's bling.

So listen closely, join the fun,
In gardens where silliness has begun.
For every bud has a tale to tell,
Of laughter and joy where nature dwells.

The Chorus of Green

In the meadow, colors collide,
Dancing daisies take it all in stride.
Chubby bumblebees buzz in glee,
Laughing at how free they can be.

Each blade of grass shakes to the beat,
Their tiny roots groove, oh so sweet!
A tune of chirps from the hidden nests,
As mama bird pecks at her sleeping guests.

The sun joins in with a bright hello,
While shadows play tag and duck below.
Each rustle of leaf brings giggles anew,
In this chorus of green, what's not to woo?

With rhythms of nature, so wacky and fun,
Under the sky, our hearts all run.
In fields where joy plants its seed,
The laughter of plants is all we need.

Echoes of Budding Dreams

Out of the soil, dreams start to sprout,
With green ambitions and a cheeky shout.
Frogs croak in chorus under the moon,
Planning a ball for the flowers in bloom.

A dandelion wishes on the breeze,
While the daisies giggle and tickle the knees.
Crickets compose a nighttime song,
As colorful petals sway along.

Butterflies prance, making silly faces,
In gardens filled with all kinds of races.
With every flap and flutter they dare,
To spread a little joy in the summer air.

The night wraps around like a cozy quilt,
While laughter and dreams are quietly built.
In the echoes of dreams, let's all unite,
In a world where growth feels just right.

Leaves in Lullaby

Hush now, little leaves, don't make a peep,
As the wind sings softly, lulling to sleep.
Branches chuckle with a gentle sway,
While stars blink back, ready to play.

Crickets snicker; it's their show,
As shadows stretch, putting on a glow.
The moon's a jester, smiling so wide,
As it casts silver beams for the leaves to glide.

A squirrel sneezes with a tiny cute puff,
Waking the flowers, saying, "That's enough!"
In the night, silliness blooms so bright,
Even the shadows giggle in delight.

So close your eyes and whisper a dream,
Let nature's laughter wrap you in a beam.
In lullabies soft, find humor and grace,
In leaves that dance in their cozy embrace.

www.ingramcontent.com/pod-product-compliance
Lightning Source LLC
Chambersburg PA
CBHW072134070526
44585CB00016B/1666